Original title:
Nectar of Knowledge

Copyright © 2025 Creative Arts Management OÜ
All rights reserved.

Author: Gabriel Kingsley
ISBN HARDBACK: 978-1-80567-042-1
ISBN PAPERBACK: 978-1-80567-122-0

The Dreamcatcher's Wisdom

In the web where thoughts can play,
Dreams giggle, slip, and sway.
A snag of wisdom, caught with care,
Like a sock lost in a lazy chair.

Old tales wrapped in twinkling light,
Whiskers twitch in the moon's bright sight.
Laughter echoes, wisdom's game,
As the stars poke fun at fame.

Chasing ideas like butterflies,
Some will twirl, and some just fly.
A hiccup here, a gleeful shout,
Who needs a map when fun's about?

So spin the yarn, and giggle loud,
Turn those frowns into a crowd.
For every thought that's out of place,
Might just end up in a funny space!

Dewdrops of Clarity

In fields of thought where flowers bloom,
Ideas dance like fairies in a room.
With each droplet that sparkles bright,
Wisdom giggles, full of delight.

A spoonful of fun, a dash of cheer,
Knowledge drips in, let's give a cheer!
Like candy rain on a sunny day,
We soak it up in a silly way.

The Orchard of Ideas

In a quirky orchard where thoughts are grown,
Apples of insight rolled out on their own.
Biting into wisdom, oh what a crunch,
Mixed with giggles in every lunch!

Peachy puns and berry bright schemes,
Harvesting laughter, feeding our dreams.
Plucking bright thoughts from branches so high,
You'll find funny truths that make you sigh.

Reviving the Spirit of Inquiry

What's that noise? A whisper, a shout!
Curiosity running around, no doubt.
Tickling questions with laughter and glee,
Turning each query into a spree!

With a hop, skip, and a pull of a thread,
We dance through puzzles, merry instead.
Light bulbs flash like fireflies at night,
Inquiring minds bring joy and delight!

The Well of Understanding

Down in the well where concepts splash,
Comedic dives create quite the splash!
Buckets of giggles poured out with care,
Every dip helps us lighten the air.

Sipping from wisdom, oh what a taste,
Swirling like whirlpools, no thought goes to waste.
Riddles bubble up with a playful grin,
Splashing the mind makes learning a win!

Elixirs of Enlightenment

In a bottle, wisdom swirls,
A mix of baffling pearls.
Shake it up, watch it fizz,
Who knew learning could be this whiz?

Spilled some on my favorite hat,
Now I ponder like a cat.
Socrates with my morning brew,
Missing socks? Blame the dew!

The Luminescent Library

In the library, lamps glow bright,
Books dance around, what a sight!
A chapter trip takes a funny turn,
Who knew fiction had so much to learn?

Whispers of pages, giggles collide,
While dusty tomes try to hide.
Chasing knowledge on a caffeine high,
My brain's a circus, oh me, oh my!

Fragrant Pages of Discovery

A whiff of science, a pinch of fun,
Mix in some maths, let's run, run, run!
Cooking recipes for the brain,
Stirring up laughter like summer rain.

Caution! Ingredients may explode,
Especially if you forget the code.
Learning's a feast, tastes sweet and wild,
Oops! That was more than just mild!

Savoring the Fruits of Curiosity

Apple of wisdom, take a bite,
Peaches of logic, pure delight.
Juicy thoughts drip, sticky and bright,
Who knew pondering could be such a sight?

Tongue-tied on knowledge, what a mix!
Bananas in algebra? Such funny tricks!
Knowledge sweets, with laughter blend,
Curiosity's a journey without end!

The Alchemy of Awareness

In a lab coat, I mix my thoughts,
With beakers of wisdom, oh what a plot!
The spills bring giggles, the fumes have flair,
Who knew learning came with a side of air?

A sprinkle of humor, a dash of wit,
Each formula stirs a laugh to fit!
With every reaction, a new joke blooms,
Awareness, it seems, is fun in the rooms.

The Mellow Ambiance of Wisdom

Sitting back in my thought-filled chair,
Comfy and cozy, with snacks to share!
The wisdom flows like chocolate fondue,
Sweet and delicious, just for you!

Laughter echoes in the quiet light,
Where ideas dance, oh what a sight!
Mellow vibes and playful talks,
Who knew wisdom could wear such socks?

Sweet Elixir of Wisdom

Pour me a glass of this sweet delight,
With bubbles of laughter that tickle just right!
Each sip is a quip, a funny old phrase,
Sipping wisdom, we're lost in a haze.

The potion swirls with sparkle and cheer,
As wisdom whispers, 'Come, my dear!'
Chortles erupt, it's wisdom's disguise,
In sweetness we find the greatest surprise.

The Honeyed Path of Thought

Wandering down this sticky lane,
Where thoughts are collected like drops of rain.
Sticky situations bring giggles galore,
Who knew wisdom could be such a chore?

With a bee buzzing jokes that sting just right,
This path is a joy, what a colorful sight!
A hop, skip, and jump through honeyed dreams,
Oh look, a wise owl! Or so it seems!

Crystals of Comprehension

In jars of wisdom, I find my way,
With every spark, I giggle and sway.
I trip on ideas, face-first in thought,
Yet every stumble's a lesson I've sought.

Each thought a gem, shiny and bright,
With laughter and joy, I take flight.
I juggle my dreams like a clown on a quest,
In the circus of learning, I'm truly blessed.

Melodies of Mental Growth

A tune in my head that's silly and sweet,
It dances around like a wiggly beet.
Notes of confusion mixed with delight,
I laugh as I ponder, oh what a sight!

The chorus of questions sings loud in my brain,
A symphony formed from the joy and the strain.
With each silly verse, my wisdom expands,
I prance through the world, with flailing hands.

Sunset over the Fields of Reflection

As the sun dips low, I ponder and tease,
Questions like fireflies dance on the breeze.
I chase after answers like a child in play,
Rolling through the grass, I giggle away.

Reflections grow longer, shadows they cast,
Wisdom's a jester, how long will it last?
In the field of my thoughts, I skip and I spin,
Finding the laughter locked deep within.

Wings of Knowledge

With wings made of paper, I soar through the air,
Chasing down thoughts that are light as a prayer.
I flap and I flounder, I giggle and glide,
In the breeze of my brain, I've nothing to hide.

These feathers of wisdom tickle my mind,
The harder I think, the funnier I find.
So I laugh through the skies, as I flutter around,
In the land of the silly, true joy can be found.

Harvest Moon of Curiosity

Under the moon, bright and round,
Questions bounce, no answers found.
Like squirrels chasing their own tails,
In this dance, excitement prevails.

Thoughts pop like popcorn, oh so loud,
In this field, we're a curious crowd.
Chasing shadows, we giggle and run,
In our quest, we've barely begun.

Eureka moments fill the air,
With quirky ideas, we don't care.
Each thought a spark, a fire ignites,
On this harvest of silly delights.

We gather the laughter and quirky lore,
Our minds are the gardens we can't ignore.
And under this moon, full of cheer,
We feast on the fun of questions, my dear.

Tasting the Palette of Ideas

With a brush and a splash, we dive in deep,
Colorful thoughts make my heart leap.
A dash of whimsy, a pinch of cheer,
Each idea served with a side of jeer.

Like jellybeans in a guessing game,
Sweet and sour, never the same.
Sampling concepts, oh what a treat,
As we dance around on our quirky feet.

Each flavor we savor, a giggle ensues,
Tasting the palette, we laugh at the blues.
With every bite, our minds take flight,
In this buffet, we're sheer delight.

So come one, come all, let's feast today,
On knowledge that's funny and often astray.
With every nibble, we grow and expand,
In this joyful buffet, hand in hand.

The Canvas of Cognitive Delights

Splash! A color, a thought in the air,
Doodling ideas with a goofy flair.
This canvas stretches, a comedic spree,
As brushstrokes dance, wild and free.

Each line a giggle, each shade a jest,
In this creativity, we are blessed.
With hues of laughter and swirls of fun,
Our masterpiece shines, second to none.

Crafting a universe where reason can play,
In the art of the mind, we go astray.
From scribbles to wonders, a whimsical flight,
On this canvas of bliss, everything's right!

So roll up your sleeves, let's color the air,
With giggles and chuckles, abandon all care.
In a world where insights and humor collide,
We create a showcase of joy and pride.

Petals in the Wind of Discovery

Petals flutter down, ideas take wing,
In the breeze, we hear laughter sing.
We chase after thoughts, like butterflies bold,
Each whimsical twist, a story unfolds.

In a garden of quirks, we're playful and spry,
Silly revelations soar up to the sky.
With every gust, our minds find new heights,
A whirl of insight, a dance of delights.

As petals twirl in this merry parade,
We weave through the follies, so unafraid.
Discovery's sweet, with a chuckle or two,
In this field of fancy, we're giggling anew.

So let's gather the blooms that float in the air,
Share silly thoughts, without a care.
For in this breeze, we find our way,
Petals of learning, brightening the day.

Harvesting the Bounty of Understanding

In fields where thoughts grow tall and bright,
I tripped on facts, what a silly sight!
I gathered trivia, basket brimming,
But dropped my brain, oh, that was dimming.

With every laugh, a lesson learned,
Like juggling eggs, my wisdom turned.
I fumbled through the mind's delight,
A whimsical chase, both day and night.

Each fruit of thought, a tasty treat,
But some were sour—makes minds retreat!
With wisdom's jam, I spread it wide,
On toast of laughter, I take my ride.

The harvest done, I dance and cheer,
With wits as sharp as a volunteer.
In fields of giggles, I'll make my stand,
And learn to juggle with a steady hand.

A Journey Through Wisdom's Grove

A stroll through trees with heads held high,
Knocking on branches, oh my, oh my!
I plucked a fruit and took a bite,
The taste of learning—it's quite a fright!

Squirrels chattered all around,
Trading tales of knowledge found.
I stumbled on a root, oh dear,
Wisdom's path is not so clear!

In shades of doubt, I sought the light,
Met a wise old owl, what a sight!
He hooted jokes, I laughed so hard,
Life's lessons wrapped in funny cards.

From tree to tree, I hopped about,
Collecting giggles, oh what a route!
With every step, a puzzle to tease,
In this funny grove, I found my keys.

The Illuminated Quest

With a flashlight of whimsy, I ventured forth,
In search of giggles, of knowledge's worth.
I stumbled on riddles, like stones in my way,
Each one I answered kept gloom at bay.

Through caves of thought, I wandered wide,
Chasing shadows where wisdom hides.
I tickled the funny bones of fate,
And danced with musings, oh what a mate!

Maps made of puns led me around,
Each turn was laughter, where joy was found.
With each new mile, wisdom grew spry,
My quest was a joke that soared through the sky.

When I reached the light, it sparkled and shone,
A treasure of giggles, I stood there alone.
With a heart full of mirth, I knew I had won,
In this journey of laughter, my quest now begun.

Whispers of the Mind's Garden

In a garden of thoughts, where veggies bloom,
I dug up some carrots, but found a broom!
Each weed of doubt, I pulled with glee,
Laughter grew wild, as bright as can be.

Petals of wisdom, so soft and sweet,
Danced in the breeze—a comedic feat.
I chatted with daisies, they told me a joke,
About clumsy bees and a silly oak.

With watering can full of giggles and dreams,
I nurtured my garden with chuckles and memes.
A sunflower winked—it had quite the style,
And shared a grin that stretched a mile!

As twilight painted the skies with fun,
I knew this garden was never done.
With whispers of laughter, my heart did sway,
In the garden of minds, I'd forever play.

The Chalice of Curiosity

A cup filled with queries so bright,
Sips of giggles with each delight.
Chasing answers like a cat chases light,
In the chatter of brainwaves, all feels right.

A swig of nonsense, a dash of cheer,
Mix it with laughter, let's make it clear.
When thoughts are jumbled, we'll persevere,
With each new riddle, we shift the gear.

Bubbles of questions, fizzing in place,
Every silly thought a curious race.
Pour it all in like a wild embrace,
In this chalice, we find our space.

Threads of Wisdom

Weaving tales with laughter's thread,
Knitting jokes in every head.
Stitching wisdom where it's led,
In this fabric, fun is spread.

A spool of quirks, it's quite the sight,
Tangled yarn sparks pure delight.
With every twist, a giggle bright,
In this tapestry, we unite.

Brews of the Mind's Infinite Garden

In the pot of thought, brew a cheer,
Tea leaves dance with giggles near.
A sprinkle of whimsy, a pinch of dear,
Sipping joy with every year.

Coffee beans whispering tales so funny,
Swirling dreams like clouds of honey.
In this garden, we find the honey,
A feast of laughter, oh so sunny.

The Secret Recipe for Growth

A dash of folly, mix with flair,
Just a hint of crazy to dare.
Stir in some giggles with love to share,
Bake it slow, happiness in the air.

A scoop of wonder, taken with glee,
Sprinkle of chaos, as wild as the sea.
With each silly step, we become free,
In this secret, we're one joyful spree.

Echoes of Ancient Knowledge

In caverns deep, the scribes would write,
Of wisdom lost, on parchment white.
They claimed a scroll could grant you flight,
If only you could read it right!

Old tomes with dust, they dance and tease,
Whispering secrets with such ease.
But when I tried, it brought me fleas,
Not quite the gems, I aimed to seize.

The owls in robes, with glasses perched,
Chirped ancient tales, the nerds researched.
Yet every fable left me lurching,
For all that wisdom was outsearching!

So here I sit, a learned fool,
Chasing knowledge around the school.
With every page, I break a rule,
But isn't that the fun, after all?

Bottled Dreams of Enlightenment

In jars of thoughts, I store my schemes,
A pickle of wisdom, or so it seems.
Each corked idea bursts at the seams,
But tastes better with some ice cream!

The label reads, 'Drink up and thrive!'
But little did I know, I'd dive
Into a swamp where thoughts contrive,
And now I struggle just to survive!

My friends all laugh, they find it grand,
While I mix potions, sticks in hand.
They say wisdom's like a rock band,
But mine's a solo with no planned.

So here's to dreams in jars of light,
With quirky flavors that spark delight.
I toast to knowledge, quirky and bright,
Let's dance in the madness of the night!

Nectarine Thoughts

A thought so juicy, plucked from the tree,
I bite real hard, it's quite sticky!
But find me a thought, sweet as can be,
Without it turning my hands all icky!

The philosophers peel back their layers,
Explaining life with zesty prayers.
Yet when I try, I'm met with glares,
And I end up munching on my cares!

With every thought I try to bake,
I mix and swirl, what a big mistake!
Instead of wisdom, I get a cake,
And realize it's just for my sake!

So here's to fruit that looks profound,
With every bite, confusion found.
I'll keep on feasting all around,
With nectarine thoughts that might astound!

The Archive of Forgotten Fruits

In dusty shelves, old fruits do dwell,
Each bittersweet with a tale to tell.
Bananas of wisdom, quite a bell,
Ringing loud, but they smell too well!

Peaches of lore, with fuzzy skin,
They giggle and wiggle, a wild spin.
But every time I try to win,
I'm left with a mushy grin!

Plums of past that burst with glee,
Expose the secrets we can't foresee.
Yet when I reach for one, oh me!
I slip and slide, and fall on my knee!

So gather round, let's have a feast,
On fruits of wisdom, to say the least.
With every bite, laughter released,
We learn and giggle, a merry beast!

The Fountain of Infinite Learning

In a garden bright with books,
I tripped and fell on learning looks.
My brain soaked up, like bread in soup,
I guess I joined the knowledge group!

I asked a tree, 'What should I know?'
It whispered truths as breezes blow.
But then it chuckled with great cheer,
'You still can't fix your lawnmower, dear!'

A cat on a shelf gave me advice,
Purring wisdom, oh so nice.
But when I sought a serious tome,
It yawned and claimed it's time for home!

So here I am, a fool in awe,
Of every wacky insight's law.
Learning's a laugh, let's take a seat,
In this crazy dance, we'll feel the beat!

Sweet Brews of Revelation

I brewed a pot of clever tea,
With hints of strange philosophy.
It bubbled up with jokes so sly,
A sip brought laughs, oh me, oh my!

The cups all smiled, they blabbed away,
'Who knew thought could taste this way?'
I spilled my drink on my new book,
And now it's just an artful look!

As sugar swirled, the thoughts grew wild,
A muffin claimed it's wisdom reconciled.
I pondered deep while munching pie,
'What is the meaning of the sky?'

So here's my toast to every brew,
Each little sip sparks something new.
With crumbs and giggles, I confess,
Learning's a treat, let's all digress!

The Crystal Chalice of Reflection

In a chalice clear, I gaze and squint,
At tangled thoughts that seem to hint.
Reflections dance like quirky sprites,
Flipping wisdom on wild flights!

A ghost of Shakespeare made me laugh,
'Your puns by now are quite the gaffe!'
Yet as I sip from dreams untold,
His sonnets sparkled, mighty bold!

A wise old frog jumped on my lap,
He croaked, 'This knowledge fits like a cap!'
But when I asked for life's grand scheme,
He leaped away, 'I lost my dream!'

So sip and ponder, dear friend,
The wacky journey has no end.
With every gulp, a laugh you'll find,
In this reflecting glass of mind!

Wings of Enlightenment

Fluttering books with feathered grace,
Knowledge birds dance in wild space.
They flap their wings, so bright and free,
Chasing ideas like honeybee!

I tried to catch one, what a feat,
It squawked and led me to a sweet.
A piece of cake and funny lore,
Who knew learning was not a chore?

With giggles wrapped in paper dreams,
Those flying thoughts burst like bright beams.
So here I sit, on clouds of fun,
With wings that take me, one by one!

So laugh, my friend, as wisdom soars,
Through skies of giggles, open doors.
For every thought that's light and free,
In this circus of minds, let's just be!

Petals of Perception

In fields of bright ideas, we roam,
With thoughts like butterflies, finding a home.
A giggle here, a chuckle there,
Wisdom sprouted, beyond compare.

In conversations like jigsaw, we play,
Connecting pieces in a quirky way.
Each thought a petal, some odd, some fine,
We dance through the garden, sipping on time.

Silly notions swirl like bees,
Buzzing about with the greatest of ease.
We tickle our brains till they giggle and laugh,
As knowledge pours out like a wacky giraffe.

So let's plant these seeds in the fertile ground,
With every wisecrack, more joy is found.
In the garden of thought, we cheerfully grow,
With petals of laughter, our knowledge will glow.

The Alchemy of Thought

In the cauldron of brain, ideas collide,
A pinch of nonsense, we lovingly guide.
With giggles and snorts, we mix and we mash,
Turning dull moments into a comedy bash.

On the table of minds, experiments brew,
In a lab coat of dreams, we're testing it too.
A beaker of wisdom, a dash of delight,
Transforming bland facts into pure comic light.

In our playful lab, we make thoughts pop,
With bubbling laughter that never won't stop.
The potion of humor, we happily sip,
As we gather round for a knowledge-filled trip.

So join in the fun, let's mix up the cream,
In the alchemy of thought, we all can dream.
With ideas exploding, like soda so spry,
Let's keep the giggles as our thoughts fly high.

The Labyrinth of Enlightened Souls

In corridors of wit, we wander around,
With signs that point 'no where' and yet they astound.
Each corner we turn, brings laughter anew,
As we trip on our thoughts and lose our shoe.

In the maze of wisdom, we play hide and seek,
With riddles that tease, and thoughts that are meek.
A twist and a turn, and what do we see?
A door marked 'crazy', come follow me!

With shadows of laughter, we dance in delight,
In this labyrinth bright, our minds take flight.
Lost? Not at all, we just roam for the fun,
Turning serious queries into jokes on the run.

So skip through the puzzle, embrace the strange,
For wisdom combined with humor will range.
In the labyrinth of souls, let's twirl and bounce,
For every wise word has a giggle to pronounce.

Harmony in the Hives of Learning

In hives of bright thinkers, we swarm all around,
With ideas that buzz, in a sweet joyful sound.
Each one a worker, with nectar to share,
As we tickle our brains with wisdom and care.

The bees make us grin with their funny little dance,
While we gather the knowledge, at every chance.
In this buzzing ballet, we ponder and play,
Creating sweet stories that brighten our day.

The hive's full of wisdom, but watch out for stings,
When theories take flight on their silly little wings.
With laughter we gather, our hearts set aglow,
In the harmony of learning, together we flow.

So join in the buzz, let's all take a flight,
In the garden of humor, where minds take delight.
With honeyed ideas and laughter so sweet,
Let's frolic in knowledge, in every heartbeat.

A Taste of Curiosity

In a jar labeled 'Wisdom', I took a big sip,
My brain did a dance, oh what a wild trip!
Fish started to chatter, and trees grew tall,
All from one gulp, I was feeling quite small.

I asked a frog for advice on my snack,
He croaked back loudly, 'There's no turning back!'
With each silly question, I got quite a jest,
Turns out my choices were none of the best.

Books flew like butterflies, oh what a sight,
They fluttered and flapped in the soft morning light.
I chased them around, trying to take notes,
But found they preferred their own little moats.

Now I plant seeds in the garden of thoughts,
Where logic and laughter are all tangly knots.
Each blossom of nonsense makes me smile wide,
Who knew that the brain was such a fun ride?

The Garden of Erudition

In a whimsical garden with flowers so bright,
I found knowledge blossoming left and right.
I picked up a fact, then it slipped from my grip,
"I swear it was here," I said with a quip.

The carrots debate where the radishes grow,
While cabbage plants argue 'bout who steals the show.
With a pinch of green humor and a dash of wit,
Learning felt easier, nothing seemed a fit.

A rusty old scarecrow shared tales of the past,
Saying, "Don't be so serious, learning's a blast!"
With each knock-knock joke, ideas took flight,
Even the worms giggled, oh what sheer delight!

In this garden of thought, each petal a clue,
Puns turned to stories, from silly to true.
I planted my questions, let them grow wild,
And suddenly wisdom felt like a playful child.

Infusions of Truth

I brewed a big pot of thoughts on the stove,
With spices of humor, a secret alcove.
I stirred in some giggles, a dash of surprise,
Then poured out the broth in a bowl of wise pies.

"Good soup," said the cat, with a wink from his eye,
"Truth tastes best served when it's topped by a lie!"
I checked the recipe; it made no sense,
Yet laughter seemed richer with every expense.

Silly debates with a spoon for a mic,
Gave rise to such stories from creatures alike.
Each line was a burp, a hiccup of joy,
Even the fish joined, a flamboyant ploy!

So I sipped on my potion of silliness brewed,
With the flavor of fun, my worries subdued.
Each bubble a lesson, each sip was the key,
Who knew that the truth could be so silly, whee!

The Luminous Distillate

In a lab where the bright ideas shine like the sun,
I mixed up some thoughts, oh what a fun run!
The test tubes giggled, each label a pun,
This science of nonsense had only begun.

I found a potion that made me dance,
And suddenly logic forgot its last chance.
Jumping conclusions like frogs from a pond,
The results were skewed, but oh, they were fond.

I asked for a sample of genius so bright,
The bottle replied with a wink and a fright!
Sipping laughter like candy, I felt so sublime,
Each bubble of wisdom, a tickle in rhyme.

So here's to the distillate of mirth-filled ideas,
Where giggles are serious and nonsense clears fears.
In this lab of delight, I'll concoct and create,
A world filled with laughter, now isn't that great?

Sipping from the Well of Insight

I dipped a cup in wisdom's well,
And slurped it down with quite a yell.
The echo laughed, the well did wink,
"Drink up, dear friend, don't stop to think!"

The bubbles popped like little brains,
Each burp unleashed profound refrains.
I learned that socks are best in pairs,
And chickens sing to mend their flares!

From quirks of life to endless puns,
A splash of jokes, my heart it runs.
So let us sip and share a cheer,
At this bright well, you'll shed a tear!

As wisdom flows like lemonade,
With every gulp, new thoughts parade.
So join the party, have a taste,
In this odd quest, there's no time waste!

A Garden of Illuminated Minds

In a garden lush with thinking blooms,
Where thoughts pop up and weave their room,
The daisies giggle, the roses grin,
While tomatoes ponder, "Where've we been?"

Each flower whispers secrets bright,
Of pondering stars and moonlit flight.
The bees take notes but hum in tune,
To brighten day from darkened noon.

A sunflower wears spectacles bold,
Sipping sunbeams – their wisdom gold.
While tulips twirl in joyous dance,
A garden party? Oh, what a chance!

So let's plant seeds of every jest,
And harvest laughs; they're always the best.
In this garden, fresh and wise,
Where insight blooms and boredom dies!

The Golden Draught of Understanding

In a tavern where the thinkers meet,
With mugs of wisdom, oh what a treat!
The golden draught flows endlessly,
Sipping laughter and antics, oh glee!

The philosophers argue with eggs on head,
While poets juggle words instead.
A toast to senses, sharp and sly,
With every gulp, we learn to fly!

They say the secret's deep within,
Just drink it down and let the fun begin!
Like ducks in suits, we waddle 'round,
Finding humor in the profound!

So raise your glass to silly thoughts,
As wisdom mingles with silly knots.
In this tavern, joy's the theme,
Drink deep, dear friend, forever dream!

Blossoms of Insight

In a world where ideas bloom,
Full of laughter and skillful zoom.
The flowers chatter, their petals bright,
Sharing knowledge with pure delight.

A dandelion bursts with facts so sweet,
While violets giggle at every beat.
The daisies offer their plucky cheer,
In this garden, wisdom's ever near!

With buzzing bees as our merry choir,
We celebrate every thought we desire.
A sprinkle of humor on every leaf,
Together we dance with disbelief!

So cultivate ideas; let them grow,
In this lively patch, all truths we sow.
Blossoms of insight, bright and fun,
Together we bask in the warmth of the sun!

Pathways of Enlightenment

In the library, I tripped on a book,
Wisdom flew by with a mischievous look.
I asked a sage for a bite-sized cheer,
He scoffed and said, "Just don't spill your beer!"

Maps of knowledge, scattered and grand,
But my brain is as full as a jar made of sand.
I tried to tweet a thought to the stars,
But my wisdom's stuck in traffic with cars.

A pumpkin taught me more than some men,
I carved a face; it grinned back again.
I painted ideas in shades of delight,
But my muse took a nap, oh, what a sight!

So here I wander, with laughter in hand,
Learning's a joke, just as I planned.
In the circus of life, where wisdom can stall,
I juggle my thoughts, and I still drop the ball!

Echoes of Culinary Wisdom

Cooking up thoughts in a pot on the stove,
But burnt my ideas, now they hardly probe.
A recipe's hidden in the depths of my fridge,
Yet all I can find is some cheese on the edge.

I boiled my dreams with a pinch of salt,
Then stirred in some errors, and added a fault.
My teacher once said, 'Just take a good bite',
But all that I tasted was leftover night.

I sautéed my fears with a dash of regret,
Diced up my doubts, but they won't let me forget.
So here on my plate sits a feast so absurd,
A few laughs and giggles, but no wise word.

So gather around, with forks and some knives,
Life's cookbook is wild, it's where chaos thrives.
Sweet moments are served; just add a few jokes,
And learn from the kitchen, where laughter provokes!

Silken Threads of Understanding

I wove a tapestry of knowledge divine,
But my needle's been missing for quite a long time.
Strands of wisdom tangled in knots,
My loom's had enough; it ties itself in spots.

A spider once whispered, "It's all in the weave,"
But when I got tangled, I just had to cleave.
I tried to sew up my thoughts in a quilt,
But each patch that I made left my patience built.

I danced with ideas, twirling and bright,
Then tripped in the dark, what a comical sight!
My threads caught on laughter, a riotous game,
Stitching silly stories, forgetting the name.

Each loop tells a tale of lessons refined,
Yet somehow, I've tangled each joke in a bind.
Still, I press on, with a grin on my face,
For the fabric of learning is a wild, silly place!

Inscriptions of Eternal Learning

In a dusty old book, I found quite a mess,
Inscriptions of wisdom wrapped in distress.
I tried to decipher the squiggles I saw,
But all I could read was, 'Just hang out with straw.'

A scroll rolled on by, with a wink and a cheer,
"Knowledge is tasty, but watch for the beer!"
I wrote down my thoughts on a napkin too free,
Now it's stuck on the fridge - my fridge's PhD.

Last night I dreamed of a wise old crow,
He cawed out secrets that I still don't know.
I chased after truths down a winding path,
But it ended up pouring with whimsical wrath.

So here's to the scholars who tumble and play,
Who find joy in learning, come what may.
For the scrolls of the ages tell stories so grand,
But the funniest tales often walk hand in hand!

Tales from the Well of Knowledge

In a well, wisdom flows, oh so deep,
But sometimes it's just tales that makes us weep.
Like the fish who thought he could fly,
Ended up wet with a puzzled sigh.

A wise old owl loved to give advice,
But his puns? Yes, they weren't very nice.
He hooted, 'Don't be a turkey, just soar!'
While we wondered what he was wise for.

Then came a parrot, bright and bold,
Claiming secrets as treasures of old.
But squawking out riddles, he'd lose his track,
Leaving all of us wondering, "What'd he say back?"

So we laugh at the lessons hidden away,
In the well where knowledge chooses to play.
It's the folly that teaches more than a book,
And each slip and fall gets us a new look.

A Symphony of Senses

Close your eyes, can you hear the hue?
Taste the sound? It's outlandish too!
A banana playing notes on a guitar,
While lemonade parades in a lemon car.

The smell of popcorn tickles your thoughts,
Mixing with sounds of jazz, oh what a lot!
A potato tap dances, so spry and spry,
While a carrot croons and almost can fly.

Hear the colors as they start to sing,
While your taste buds prepare for a zing.
Tomatoes do waltzes, quite off the beat,
Causing giggles for everyone's treat.

In this odd world where senses collide,
We find that each moment, we laugh and abide.
For in every mix-up, there's a grand key,
To unlock the fun of just being free.

The Cauldron of Cognition

A witch in the woods brews thoughts in a pot,
Making a stew of ideas, quite a lot.
She adds a dash of giggles, a pinch of dreams,
And stirs with a broomstick—how silly it seems!

Her cat spills the beans, oh what a whisker,
With each leap and bound, he becomes a jester.
"Knowledge," he purrs, "is not just for the wise,
But also for those who wear pies as disguise!"

A lad in a cap stumbles into the scene,
Tripping on wisdom like it's made of whipped cream.
"Is this all a game?" he questions out loud,
As the cauldron bubbles and gathers a crowd.

In this bubbling brew, we all find a laugh,
With each silly thought, a divided path.
For knowledge is light, and when mixed with jest,
It's not just for tests, it's truly the best!

Gathering the Fruits of Psyche

In the orchard of thoughts, we gather in glee,
Plucking ideas like apples from a tree.
One red says, "Eat me, I'm juicy and bright!"
While a green one retorts, "I'm sour, what a fright!"

A peach rolls by, sporting a giggle or two,
Saying, "Hey there, buddy, how 'bout a chew?"
But beware of the prune, so wrinkled and wise,
Offering truths wrapped up in surprise.

Beneath a big grape, shadows dance with flair,
Spinning tales of knowledge, light as the air.
"Take a bite!" they cheer, "And savor the taste,
Each fruit holds a secret—don't let it go to waste!"

So we munch with joy, stuffing our minds,
In this playful orchard, laughter unwinds.
For wisdom is sweeter when shared with a chuckle,
In the garden of thoughts, let joy be our buckle.

The Fragrance of Intellectual Blossoms

In a garden where ideas bloom,
The flowers giggle, dispelling gloom.
One says, "I'm brighter than the sun!"
Another replies, "But I'm much more fun!"

They dance in circles, sharing a tale,
Of wisdom found in a gusty gale.
"What's the best fruit?" a daisy remarks,
"Bananas! They make the silliest sparks!"

The bees are buzzing, quite in a daze,
Sipping on thoughts through a sweet, silly haze.
"Why learn to fly when you can just sit?"
One flower chuckles, "This is quite a hit!"

So wander among these blooms so bright,
Grab a smile, and hold on tight.
For laughter here fuels the mind,
And the silliest ideas are the best kinds!

Raindrops of Reflection

When raindrops fall, they bring a cheer,
Each puddle holds a thought sincere.
One drops in, "Am I just a splash?"
Another says, "You're more than a dash!"

They splatter wisdom on the street,
Each ripple makes the moments sweet.
"What's under your cap?" a raindrop grins,
"Just a tad of hope where silliness begins!"

With every bounce, they giggle aloud,
In the dance of drops, they're a happy crowd.
"A shower of thoughts is what we need!"
As puddles become the minds we feed!

So come and jump in with glee and fun,
Splashing around till the day is done.
Through drops of laughter, we'll all see,
Reflections reveal just who we can be!

Enchanted Pages Beneath the Stars

In a library under twinkling skies,
The books converse with sparkling eyes.
One whispers, "I've seen the world's best blunder!"
Another laughs, "I've got tales like thunder!"

They flip their pages, oh what delight,
Sharing laughs into the night.
"Did you hear the tale of the cat so sly?"
"It thought it could just reach the sky!"

With every chapter, the giggles swell,
Words become wizards, casting their spell.
"Why read alone when friends can join?"
In this bookish world, there's much to enjoy!

So gather your pals and dive in deep,
Through tales of joy and laughter to keep.
Beneath the stars, let the fun unfold,
For knowledge is sweet when shared and bold!

Tasting the Honey of Insight

In a hive where wisdom's stored,
The bees just can't help but hoard.
One buzzes, "I've got a secret to share!"
Another says, "Do we need more air?"

They sip on thoughts, so sticky and sweet,
Crafting ideas that can't be beat.
"What's the best flavor?" a bee takes a sip,
"Silly giggles—they give you quite a trip!"

So they buzz around, spreading delight,
As honey drips in the warm sunlight.
"Life's a picnic, folks! Let's have a feast!"
With laughter and joy, they say, "To say the least!"

So gather 'round and join in the fun,
With the sweetness of knowledge, we will run.
Through laughter and honey, our minds take flight,
Together we shine, oh what a sight!

Chasing the Fireflies of Thought

In a field where ideas flicker bright,
I chased them all through the starry night.
They giggle and twirl like kids at play,
But vanish like candy at the end of the day.

I caught one once, it tickled my brain,
And made me wonder if cows can complain.
The fireflies laughed, oh what a sight,
As I danced with my thoughts, in sheer delight.

With jars in hand like a quirky bee,
I trapped my thoughts, but they giggled with glee.
They escaped in a cloud of shimmering light,
Leaving me pondering through the long, dark night.

So off I pranced, with my jar now bare,
Swapping wisdom like it's the latest fair.
Each thought a firefly, a tickling tease,
Learning's a party, so join me, if you please!

The Symphony of Intellectual Flavors

In the kitchen of ideas, I stir the pot,
Mixing sweet dreams with a dash of thought.
There's chocolate of wisdom, and spicy wit,
A pinch of humor, the perfect fit.

I sauté the facts, let them simmer down,
While comedy sprinkles like glittery brown.
Baked logic rises, so fluffy and light,
Taste it while it's fresh, it's sheer delight!

A buffet of learning, with all-you-can-eat,
I dabble on dishes that can't be beat.
With laughter and quirkiness on each plate,
Join me for a meal that will celebrate!

So fork in hand, let's dig right in,
There's no room for boredom, we want to win.
Feasting on flavors of curious bliss,
In this brainy kitchen, you'll not want to miss!

Aroma of the Mind's Harvest

In fields of wisdom, I plant my seeds,
Watering thoughts, pulling pesky weeds.
An aroma so sweet, it fills the air,
With giggles of knowledge, a whimsical flair.

The harvest comes in, oh what a sight,
Tomatoes of trivia, carrots of fright.
I pluck and I taste, oh what a blend,
Each bite brings laughter, my brain's best friend.

Preserving my bounty in jars with a grin,
I trade with my pals, what a joyous win!
"Here's some insight, may I have a thought?"
With each quirky exchange, I'm never distraught.

So gather around this garden of cheer,
And munch on the fruits of our labor here.
With every chuckle, we sow and we reap,
The harvest of laughter, a treasure to keep!

Mandalas of Learning

In circles of thought, I spin to delight,
Creating a pattern, both silly and bright.
With crayons of wisdom, I scribble away,
A mandala of learning, come join in the play!

Each twist is a lesson, a loop is a plan,
With funky designs, I spark up the clan.
The colors of knowledge swirl round and round,
In this wacky creation, true joy can be found.

From doodles of history to squiggles of maths,
I laugh at the puzzles and search for the paths.
When things get tricky, I giggle and cheer,
Who knew learning could be so sincere?

So grab your own crayon, let's create and explore,
A whirlpool of wisdom, we'll ask for more.
For in these designs, oh so funny and bright,
Are the secrets of joy and the spark of insight!

The Fountain of Learning

In a garden where wisdom grows,
Laughter flows like a river, you know.
A squirrel with a book on its head,
Says, "You learn best when you're well fed!"

A chicken crossed the street today,
With a riddle that made me sway.
"Why did it walk, with a strut and a shout?"
I laughed so hard, I just fell out!

A fountain spouts facts like confetti,
Splashing knowledge, oh so petty.
I slipped on a thought and took a dive,
Came up with ideas that really thrive!

So dance by the water, and join the fun,
Learning's a party, for everyone!
With giggles and grins, we'll all take a dip,
In the fountain of learning, let's make a trip!

Petals of Perception

In a field where ideas bloom,
A bee says, "Stop! Don't bring the gloom!"
He sips from the petals, with a wink and a buzz,
"Knowledge is sweeter than the best fuzz!"

A flower whispered a thought so grand,
"Pick me, I'm the smartest in this land!"
But when I picked, it sneezed a lot,
And I learned that flowers can be quite hot!

The daisies spun in a joyful whirl,
With facts that make my head twirl!
"I once knew a cat who played the lute,
But all he learned were songs about fruit!"

So let's dance among the vibrant hues,
Fueling our minds with ridiculous views.
With petals of laughter in every direction,
Life's a garden of odd reflection!

The Scrolls of Illumination

In a library where secrets hide,
Scrolls start to giggle, oh what a ride!
One whispered, "Reading's like a treat,
But who needs a meal when knowledge is sweet?"

A wise old owl perched on a shelf,
Said, "Don't take yourself too seriously, elf!"
For a chuckle and grin go a long way,
Even when learning leads us astray!

The scrolls rolled out some jests and quirks,
Like a historian who worked in jerks!
He wrote of kings with silly crowns,
And queens who traded their golden gowns!

So open the scrolls, take a peek,
Let laughter be what you seek!
For in the world of history's blend,
Every chapter's a giggle to send!

Elixirs of Thought

In a lab full of bubbling brews,
A mad scientist shouts, "I've got news!"
With potions that fizz and sparkle bright,
We'll raise our minds to dizzying heights!

One flask claimed to boost your brain,
But it smelled like rotten, stinky grain.
Sipped a drop, I felt so spry,
But then I sneezed and said goodbye!

A tonic for giggles, oh so rare,
It made us all bounce and twirl in the air!
"Who needs a cure for a common cold?
When laughter's the magic worth more than gold?"

So let's mix our thoughts and stir with glee,
In a potion of fun, come drink with me!
For the elixirs of thought will never betray,
As long as we're laughing along the way!

Recipes of Realization

In a pot of ponder, stir your dreams,
Add a pinch of folly, bursting at the seams.
Toss in the chaos, a dash of delight,
Simmer with laughter, from morning till night.

Whisk away doubt, turn up the heat,
Scoop out the wisdom, oh what a treat!
Garnish with humor, serve with a smile,
A feast for the mind, it's worth your while.

Bake your plans in a silly old tin,
Watch as they rise, let the fun begin!
Slice up the moments, sprinkle with cheer,
Eat up the lessons, season your year.

So grab a fork, let's dig right in,
What joy in the mess, what a raucous win!
With every bite, may you find your way,
Cooking up knowledge, day after day.

The Ambrosial Archive

In a library nook where the giggles abound,
Reside dusty books, some upside down.
Open one wide, let the pages spill,
Woops! A bubble of truth pops - what a thrill!

Each chapter a hiccup, each margin a tease,
Sipping on wisdom that flows like a breeze.
Filled with mishaps, yet rich in delight,
Who knew that knowledge could take such flight?

The spine creaks with laughter, the index knows best,
Flip through the humor, put your mind to rest.
A surprising recipe for wit and for glee,
In the Ambrosial Archive, come read with me!

So don your best glasses, the thick ones, just right,
Dive into nonsense, it's quite a sight!
Turn the pages gently, with a wink and a nod,
Knowledge is best served when it's a bit odd.

Harvesting Insights

In the garden of brain, let's plant silly seeds,
Water them daily with curious deeds.
Pull up the veggies, they're funny and bright,
Harvesting insights beneath the moonlight.

Tomatoes of thought and cucumbers fine,
Sprinkle with laughter, a gourmet design.
Toss in some puzzlers, and a jest or two,
Sauté with a sprinkle of things that are new.

Gather your pals for a whimsical feast,
Chop it all up, share a tasty beast.
With each crunchy bite, may hilarity flow,
Harvesting insights, the best way to grow!

So wear your big hat and gather the best,
Find joy in the mess, we're on a fun quest!
Let's share our delights, make memories sweet,
In the orchard of laughter, our hearts shall meet.

The Brew of Intellect

In a cauldron of thought, add a splash of jest,
Stir it all up, now we're feeling blessed!
Pour in some whimsy, a sprinkle of spice,
The brew of bright minds will surely suffice.

Heat it with giggles, let the bubbles rise,
A potion of insight, delightful surprise!
Sip from the chalice, don't be a fool,
The recipe's wacky, but it's oh-so-cool!

Chop up some laughter, mix in some fun,
Infuse with the stories that tickle and run.
With every warm sip, let the chuckles flow,
In this brew of intellect, there's more to know.

So gather 'round friends, let's share this cheer,
With cups clinking softly, here's to the year!
Drink deep of the joy, let the lessons unfold,
In the Brew of Intellect, be brave and be bold!

The Sweetness of Discovery

In a world of books and scrolls,
I search for wisdom like a troll.
With glasses perched upon my nose,
I giggle at what I propose.

I taste the facts, a curious bite,
Sipping knowledge late each night.
My friends think I'm a bit absurd,
But I'm just munching on the word!

With every page I start to feast,
A banquet filled with learning beats.
I trip on thoughts like silly cheese,
And laugh so hard, I get the sneezes!

So raise a mug of mental juice,
Let's party hard, not let it loose!
For every laugh and wit-filled phrase,
Might just set our minds ablaze.

Brews of Understanding

I brewed a pot of thoughts today,
Stirred in questions, hip-hip-hooray!
A sprinkle of wisdom, a dash of fun,
My brain is buzzing, oh what a run!

With coffee cups and tea like storms,
I sip and ponder, in strange forms.
Each gulp a giggle, each swallow a grin,
My head's a carnival, let the games begin!

Like a chef, I mix the senses,
Adding humor to the defenses.
Caution: may cause fits of glee,
Understanding's wild as the deep blue sea!

So let's raise our mugs to thought and cheer,
In this brew, the fun is near.
Let's giggle at facts and chuckle at dreams,
Pouring laughter in reality's streams.

The Golden Ambrosia

I found a jar of golden gleam,
Filled with ideas like a dream.
I dipped my spoon with grand delight,
And slurped up wisdom late at night.

A drip on toast, oh what a sight,
It tickled my brain and took to flight.
With every bite, I chuckled loud,
Who knew learning made you proud?

The taste of facts, a zing of zest,
In this feast, I am the guest.
As I twirl through thoughts like a dance,
I laugh so hard, I drop my pants!

So come and savor this sweet delight,
With friends beside, the future's bright.
Let's spoon together, share the fun,
In this golden joy, we're never done.

Flavors of the Mind

I wandered through a flavor town,
Where wisdom wears a funny crown.
Each corner turned, a taste surprise,
With every bite, it opens eyes!

Like candy canes of history,
Sweet and sour, a tasty mystery.
With laughter dripping from each treat,
Every thought's a tasty feat!

I nibble rounds of silly clues,
And chase them down with crazy snooze.
In the buffet of the mind, we play,
Grabbing laughter, come what may!

So let's take bites, share a grin,
The flavors swirl, let fun begin.
For life's a feast, don't you agree?
With every laugh, we're surely free!

Encounters with Epiphanies

In a land of ideas where thoughts get a drink,
I tripped on a notion, stopped just to think.
The lightbulbs all flickered, they danced on the page,
As wisdom slipped out, like a bird from its cage.

I met a wise owl with glasses so thick,
He hooted and chuckled, 'Come learn my quick trick!'
He served up some laughter with side dishes wise,
Each giggle a morsel, oh what a surprise!

In corners of classrooms, where chaos can freeze,
I found a few kernels, like peanuts with cheese.
Each chuckle ignited a spark in my brain,
I dined on the humor, no worry, no pain.

So here's to the journey, the laughter it brings,
With every new insight, my heart really sings.
I raise up my cup, filled with nonsense and cheer,
For every bright moment, I hold oh so dear.

The Spell of Scholarly Sips

There's magic in books, with their potions and spells,
Each page that I turn, another tall tale tells.
I sipped from the chalice of giggles and glee,
With each funny footnote, I danced like a bee.

The coffee was brewing, it sparkled with wit,
I poured me a cup, man, the wisdom was lit!
With each little gulp, enlightenment bloomed,
I snorted and snickered as knowledge resumed.

Some folks take their tea with a dash of the sly,
While others add snickers, oh my, oh my!
The scholars all gather around tables of fun,
Their laughter like bubbles, it never is done.

So fill up your mug, let the whimsy begin,
With jokes and with jests, let the learning sink in.
We'll toast to the moments where laughter holds sway,
As we sip on the saga of bright, silly play.

The Sweetness of Mindful Moments

In the garden of giggles, I pause and I snack,
On wisdom's ripe fruit, never too far back.
The apples of laughter hang low on the trees,
Each bite brings a chuckle, as sweet as you please.

Like jelly on toast, thought spreads in delight,
I munch on the moments, from morning to night.
With every kooky thought that tickles my mind,
I feast on the whimsy and feel so refined.

A sprinkle of joy goes a long, long way,
In the dessert of learning, come join the parade!
With each silly question, a slice of the pie,
I relish the sweetness, oh me, oh my!

So let's gather around, with friends near and far,
As we nibble on nonsense and feel like a star.
For the fun in the learning is the icing on top,
Together we flourish, we never will stop.

Treasures Beneath the Surface of Thought

With a shovel of laughter, I dig down so deep,
To unearth all the gems where the thinkers all creep.
I found a few giggles, some wisdom in jars,
Each chuckle a bauble, like candy from Mars.

In the caverns of notion, with echoes of cheer,
A treasure map sprawls, marked with giggles, oh dear!
I followed the breadcrumbs, each funny little clue,
And laughed as I gathered, oh how I accrue!

Some riches are silly, like socks with a tale,
While others show wisdom like cheese on a scale.
Each shiny insight, a trinket to keep,
While I dance with the knowledge, I giggle, not weep.

So here's to the quest, with treasure in sight,
For the finds that delight will keep spirits so bright.
Let's dig through the muck, find the gems that we've got,

For laughter and learning are treasures, like pot!

The Elixir of Wisdom

In a jar on the shelf, it sits with glee,
Fuzzy thoughts buzzing, like a bumblebee.
Take a sip, it's quite the spree,
But don't blame me if you start to see!

Spilled a drop, it's quite the mess,
Found a secret or maybe less?
Chased a thought, it ran, no stress,
Now I'm left in a state of guess!

Elixirs bubbling in brain's cauldron,
Mixing ideas, oh what fun!
But wisdom's fickle, like a runaway gun,
I thought I knew, but now I shun.

So let's toast to sips, a merry cheer,
To giggles and laughs, and not a tear!
For in this brew, every mind is near,
Just don't drink too much, or you'll disappear!

Whispers of Enlightenment

A whisper floats, so sweet and sly,
Like a pie in the oven, oh my, oh my!
Chasing thoughts that flutter and fly,
Like balloons at a party, reaching the sky!

Hearken closely, a giggle's tone,
The wise old owl now laughs alone.
With riddles wrapped in honeycomb,
Yet somehow I still forget my phone.

Grab the whispers, they tease your mind,
With every chuckle, new truths you'll find.
But wait a minute, was I ever blind?
To all those gems I left behind?

So here we sit, in a chatty hum,
With thoughts so sweet, they might make you numb.
Lessons learned? Or just a fun drum?
Either way, my brain's a happy glum!

The Honeyed Pages

Oh, the pages sticky, oh what a sight,
Words dance and giggle, in morning light.
They taste like laughter, oh what delight,
Just don't read too fast, or you might take flight!

A bookworm munching, lost in a trance,
Every line's a witty little dance.
Laughing at wisdom, oh what a chance,
But now I'm stuck in a wild romance!

Every point is sweet, every pun divine,
Sipping from chapters, oh how they shine.
But if I fall asleep, please don't opine,
I dream of knowledge, and it tastes like wine!

So let's read together, bring snacks if you dare,
And plunge into pages, with giggles to share.
For honey's nice, but laughter's more rare,
In our funny book's sweet, wild affair!

Sips from the Chalice of Insight

A chalice so grand, perched up high,
Filled with musings that tickle the sky.
One sip in, I'm ready to fly,
Wait, was that a dog? Oh my, oh my!

Insights bubble like a fizzy pop,
Thoughts cascading, never a flop.
Each giggle and gasp makes my brainstop,
Now I'm not sure if I'm a thinker or crop!

Yet in this chalice, wisdom does beckon,
But first, let's take a moment for reck'n.
Juggling lightbulbs, oh, what a second—
Is it clarity gained, or humor's reflection?

So here's to sips from this wacky cup,
Let's dive into laughter, and never give up!
For each chuckle shared, we fill our cup,
In this playful quest, our minds erupt!

Tasting the Essence of Learning

In dusty books, I found some cheese,
A recipe for brainy peas!
I mixed them up with jokes and puns,
Now wisdom's served with lots of fun!

With every bite, my mind expands,
Like jellybeans in eager hands.
Imagine thoughts on roller skates,
They giggle, jump, and celebrate!

Each lesson learned, a slice of pie,
In class, I'm King, oh my, oh my!
Catch the knowledge like a beach ball,
And bounce it highest of them all!

So grab your fork, let's savor more,
Each bite delights, we can't ignore!
Together we'll make hungry minds,
With wisdom's feast, we've hit the finds!

The Ambrosia of Discovery

On surfboards made of paper waves,
We surfed the sea of facts like caves.
With every ride, a silly spill,
But up we pop, oh what a thrill!

The treasure map is drawn in crayon,
X marks the spot where brains are playin'.
Digging deep in sandy thoughts,
We're pirates of what knowledge sought!

A spoonful makes the lessons sweet,
But watch out for that learning treat!
With giggles and a side of fries,
We munch on truths beneath the skies!

So raise a glass of lemonade,
To strange ideas that we have made!
In wacky hats, we boldly declare,
Discovery's fun beyond compare!

In the Orchard of Ideas

In an orchard full of wacky dreams,
Where apples giggle and bubble beams.
Plucking thoughts like fruity slogans,
Juicy surprises, oh what logins!

The lemons yell their sour plight,
While cherries dance in pure delight.
Each branch a quiz, each root a jest,
Nature's humor, it's the best!

Gather 'round the pie of learn,
With each slice, our brains will churn.
Peach pits hold secrets, hidden and round,
Crack them open for laughs abound!

So let's parade in fruity hats,
While we debate the subject of cats!
In this orchard, minds will frolic,
Fruitful giggles, truly symbolic!

The Dewdrops of Intellect

Waking up to morning light,
Dewdrops spark like dreams in flight.
Each glisten holds a quirky fact,
Knowledge hides in laughter's pact.

With silly hats and boots on feet,
We chase the thoughts, oh what a feat!
Dancing through a maze of clues,
Found the answer in my shoes!

Whispers float like petals bright,
Tickling brains with pure delight.
In the garden where all things grow,
Ideas blossom, steal the show!

So catch the droplets, sip them slow,
Let fun and learning help you grow!
For in each drop, a tale will glide,
With giggles, joy, we'll take in stride!

www.ingramcontent.com/pod-product-compliance
Lightning Source LLC
Chambersburg PA
CBHW071849160426
43209CB00003B/483